tiny

EXTREME

coloring

by Fiona Joyner

◎◦•◎◦•◎◦•◎◦•

Book 1: Lil' Oceans

To all of the art teachers who remind the students to dream. And to all of the dreamers who take the advice literally.

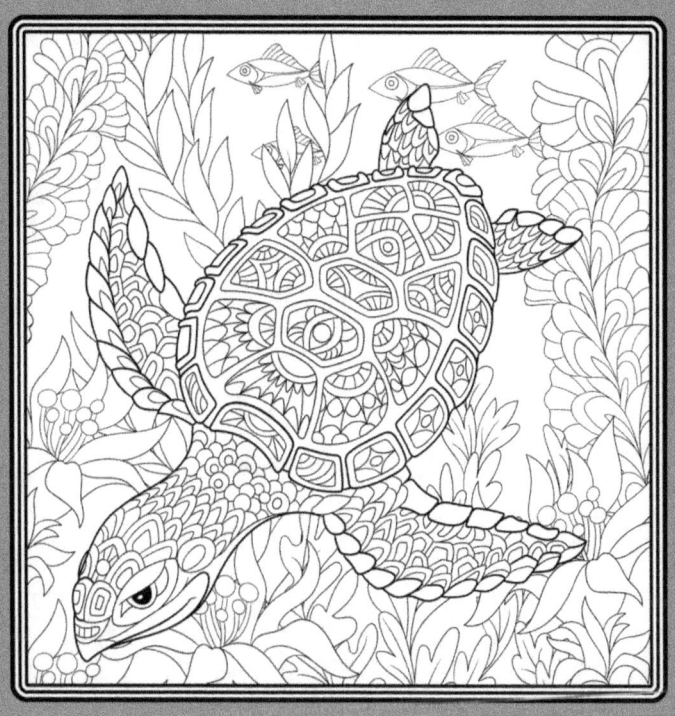

"If you can see your path laid out in front of you step by step, you know it's not your path. Your own path you make with every step you take. That's why it's your path."

--Joseph Campbell

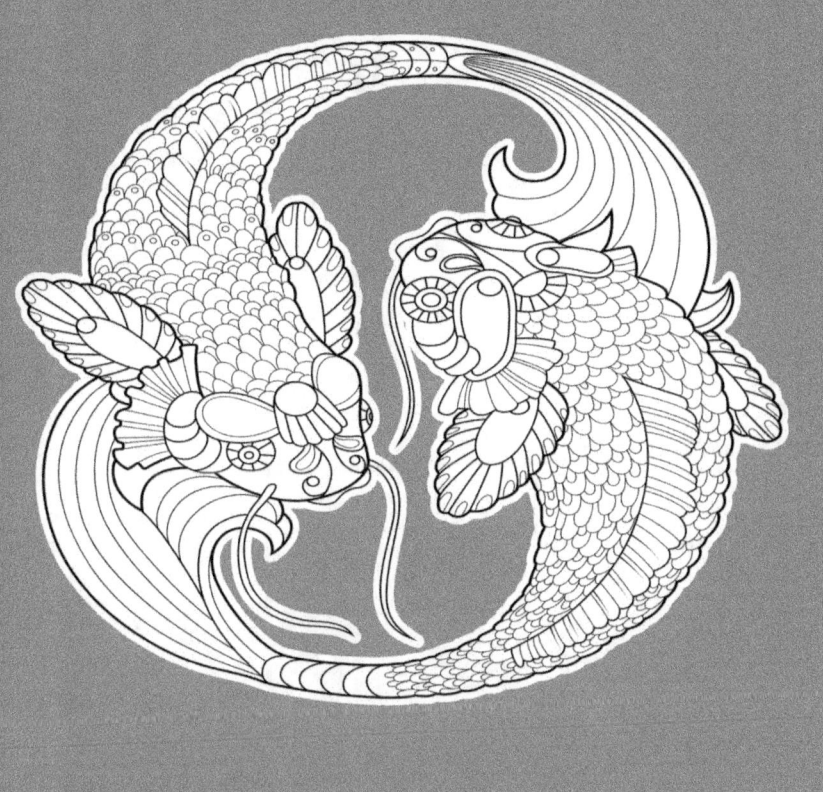

"I am not eccentric. It's just that I am more alive than most people. I am an unpopular electric eel set in a pond of catfish."

--Edith Sitwell

"The sky never falls with the rain. It is never weighed down by all that it carries. It takes all of its anchors and turns them into stars. Learn from this."

--D. Antoinette Foy

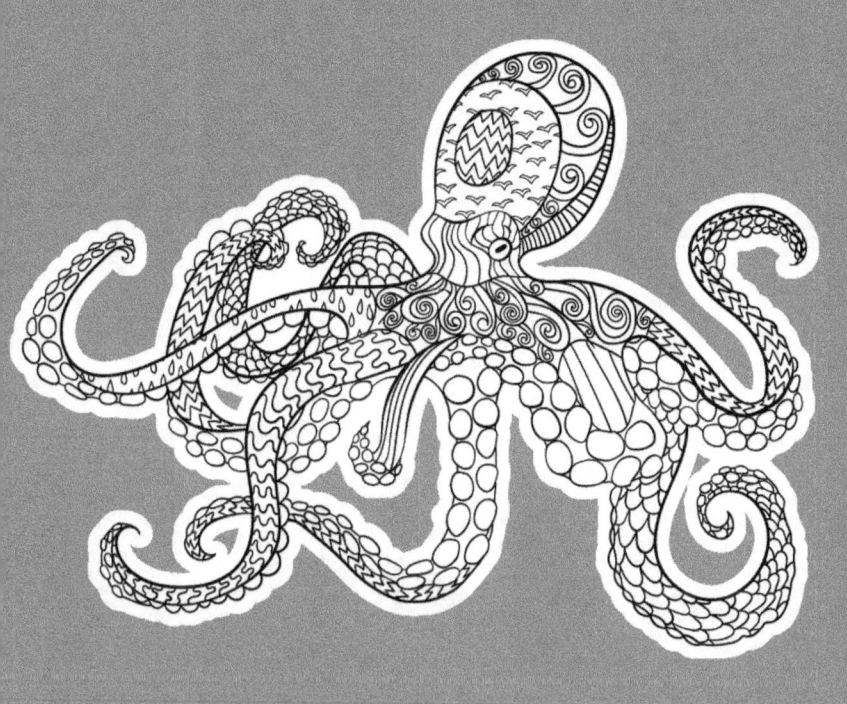

"A certain type of perfection can only be realized through a limitless accumulation of the imperfect."

--Haruki Murakami

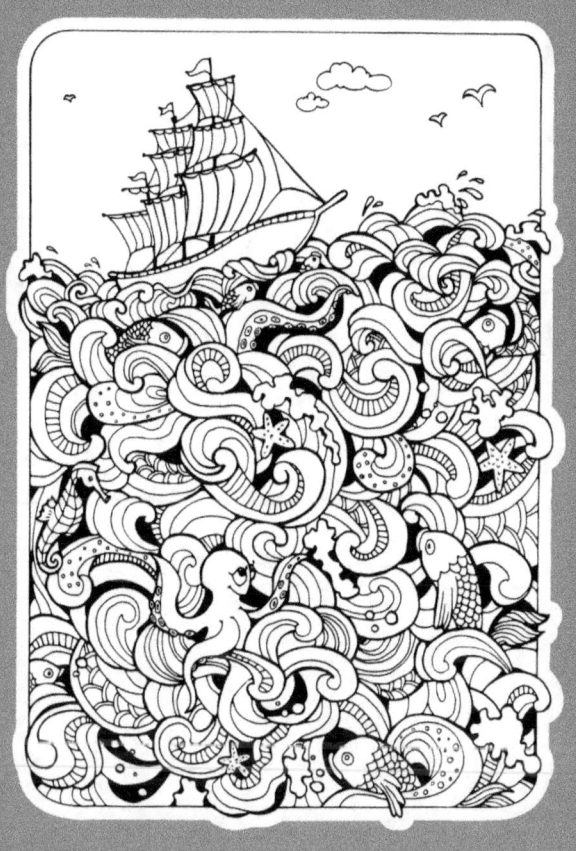

"If the highest aim of a captain were to preserve his ship, he would keep it in port forever."

--Thomas Aquinas

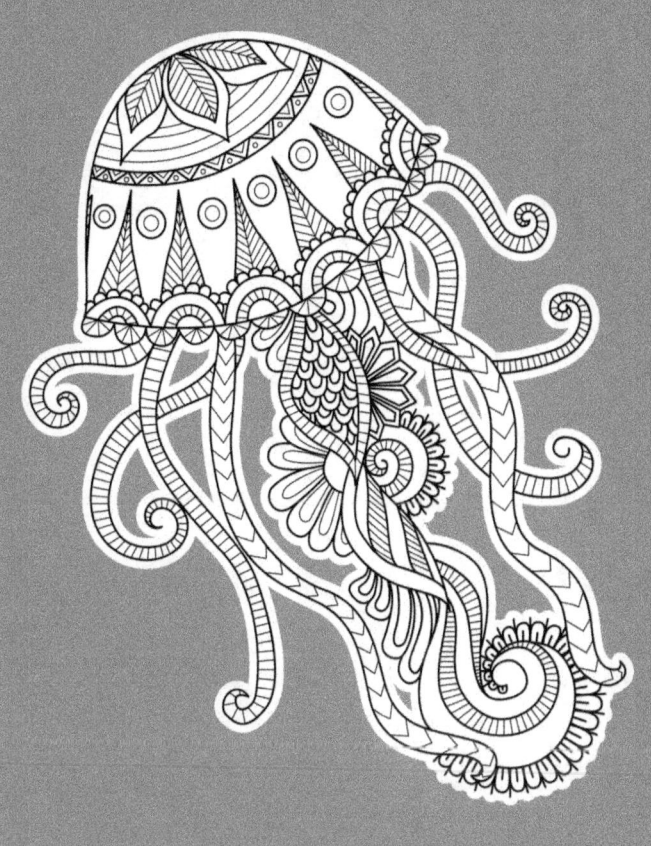

"When you live your life with an appreciation of coincidences and their meanings, you connect with the underlying field of infinite possibilities."

--William James

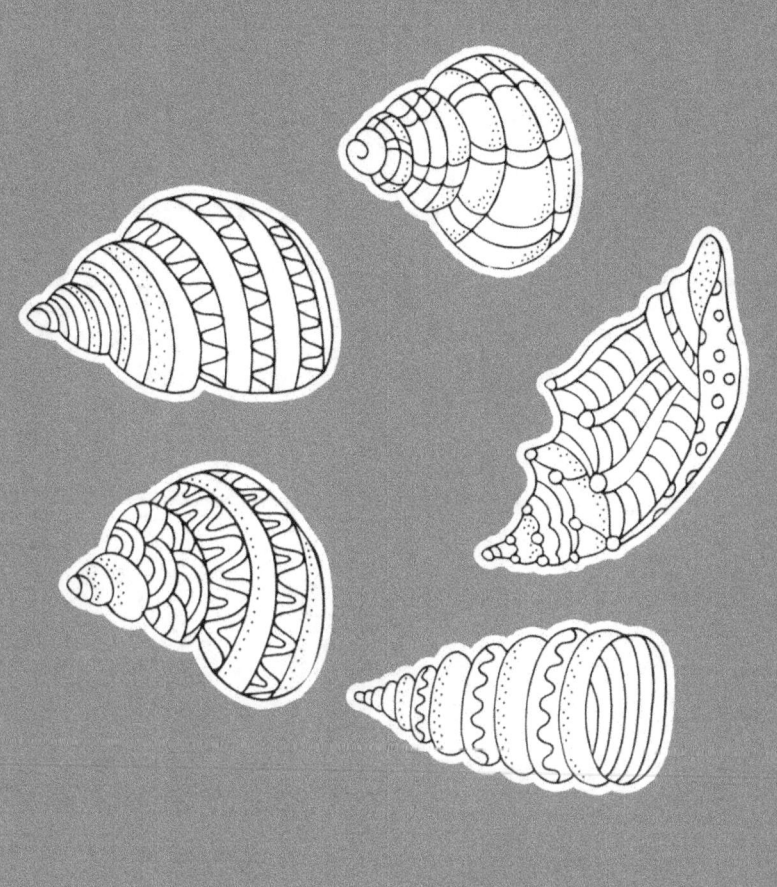

"There is one spectacle grander than the sea, that is the sky; there is one spectacle grander than the sky, that is the interior of the soul."

--Victor Hugo

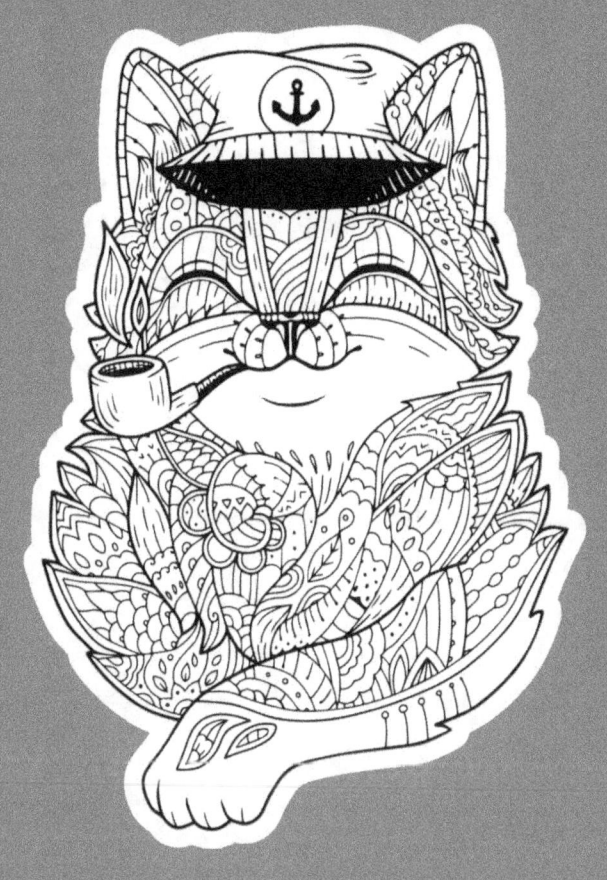

"It takes a great deal of bravery to stand up to our enemies, but just as much to stand up to our friends."

--J.K. Rowling

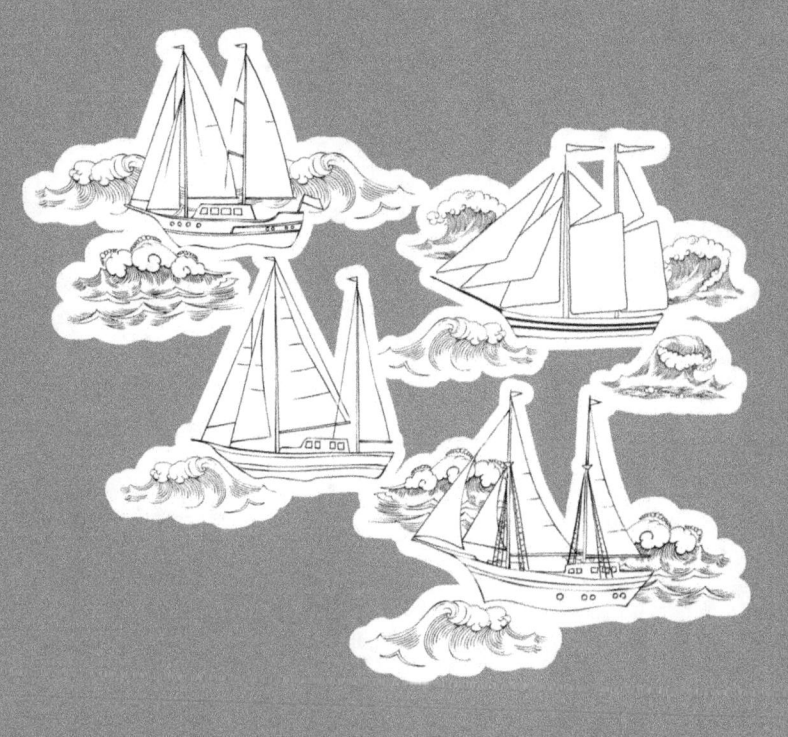

"It does not matter how slowly you go as long as you do not stop."

--Confucius

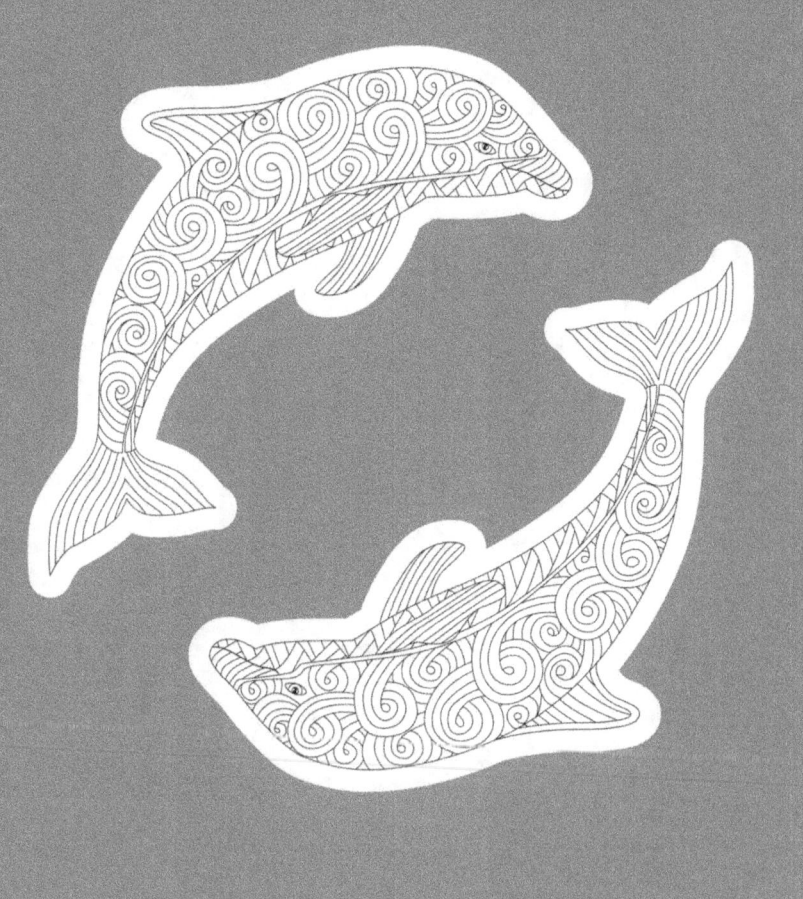

"Always   remember   that you are absolutely unique. Just like everyone else."

--Margaret Mead

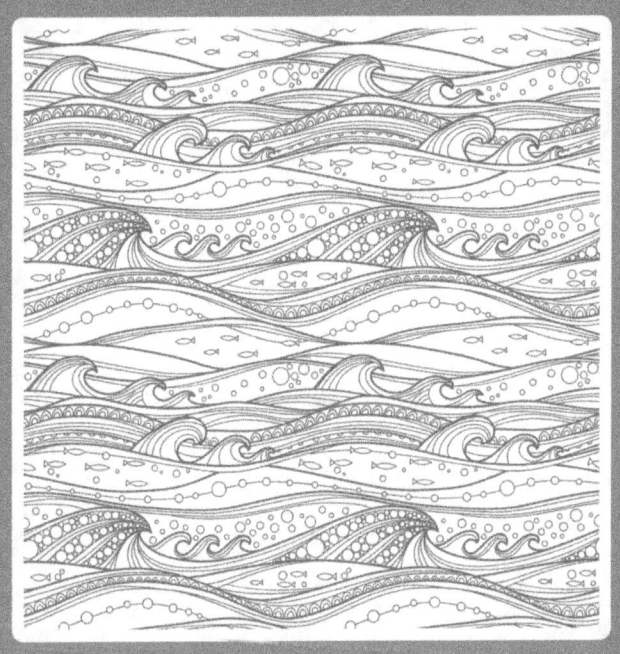

"Consider the subtleness of the sea; how its most dreaded creatures glide under water, unapparent for the most part, and treacherously hidden beneath the loveliest tints of azure."

--Herman Melville

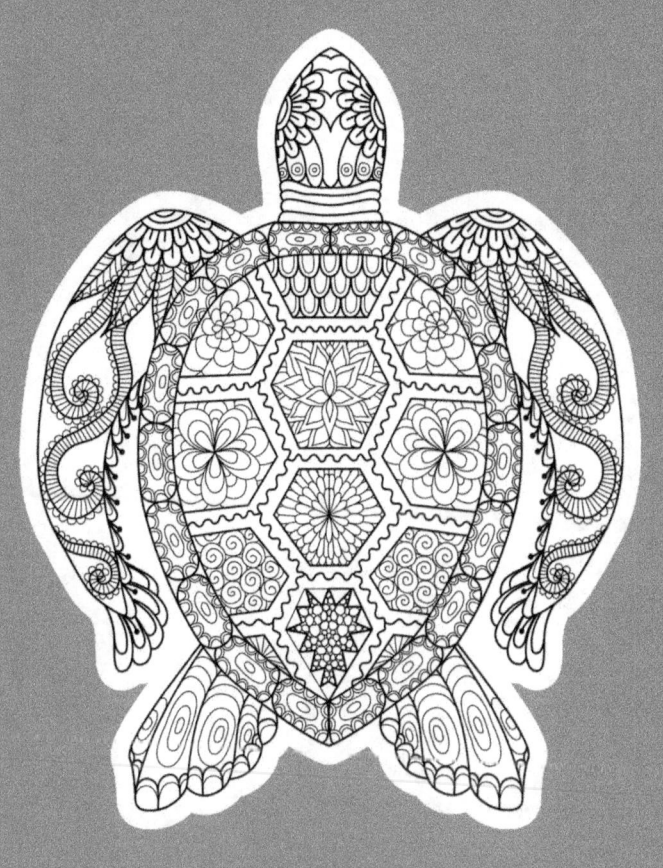

"I may not have gone where I intended to go, but I think I have ended up where I needed to be."

--Douglas Adams

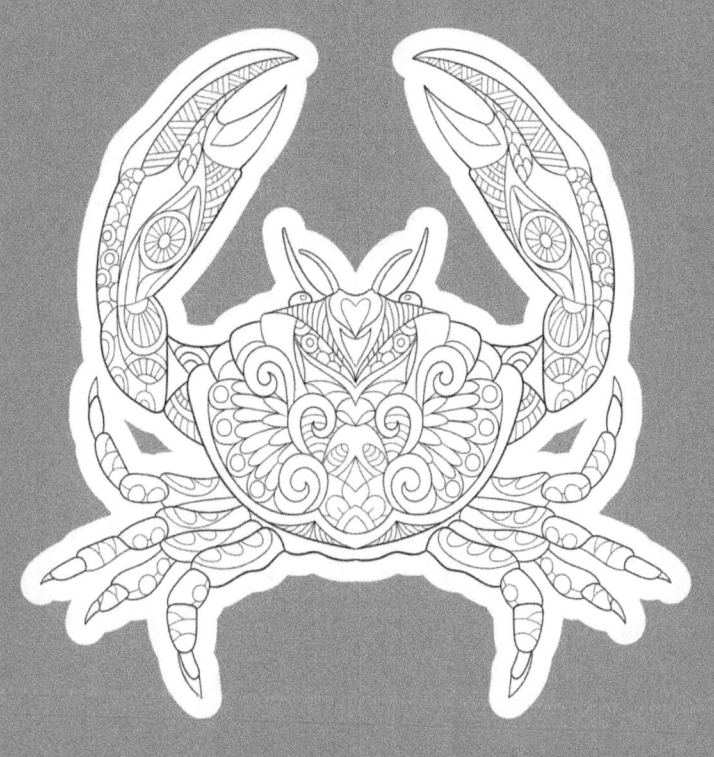

"Instructions for living a life.
Pay attention.
Be astonished.
Tell about it."

--Mary Oliver

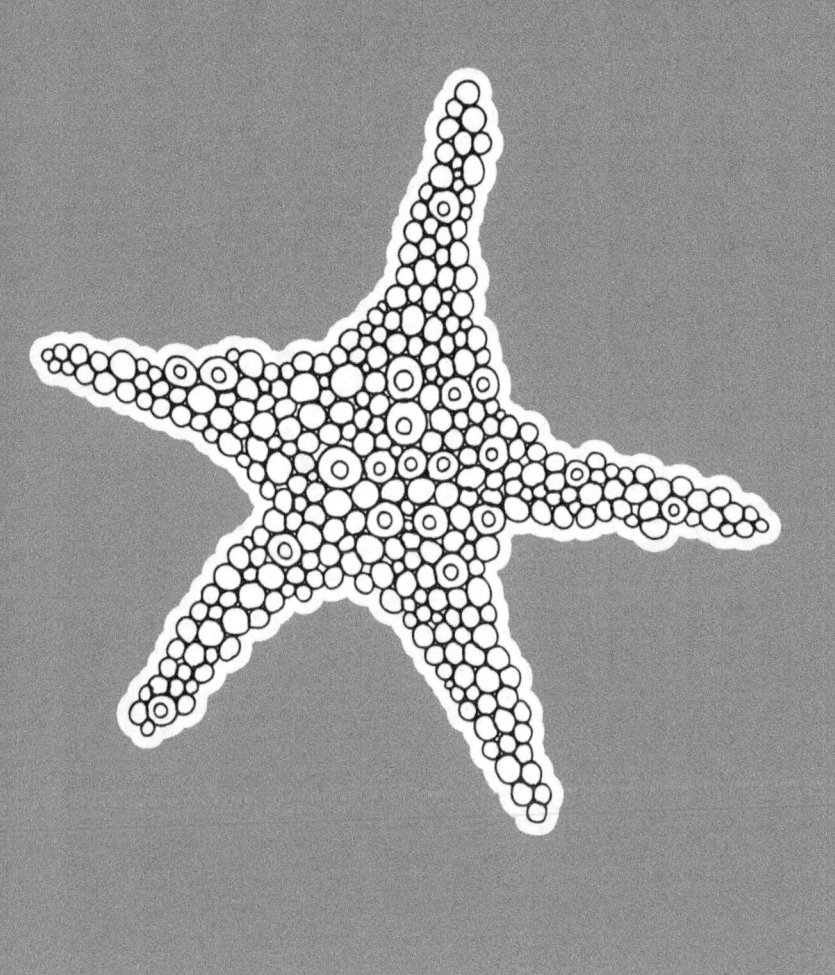

"Without ambition one starts nothing. Without work one finishes nothing. The prize will not be sent to you. You have to win it."

--Ralph Waldo Emerson

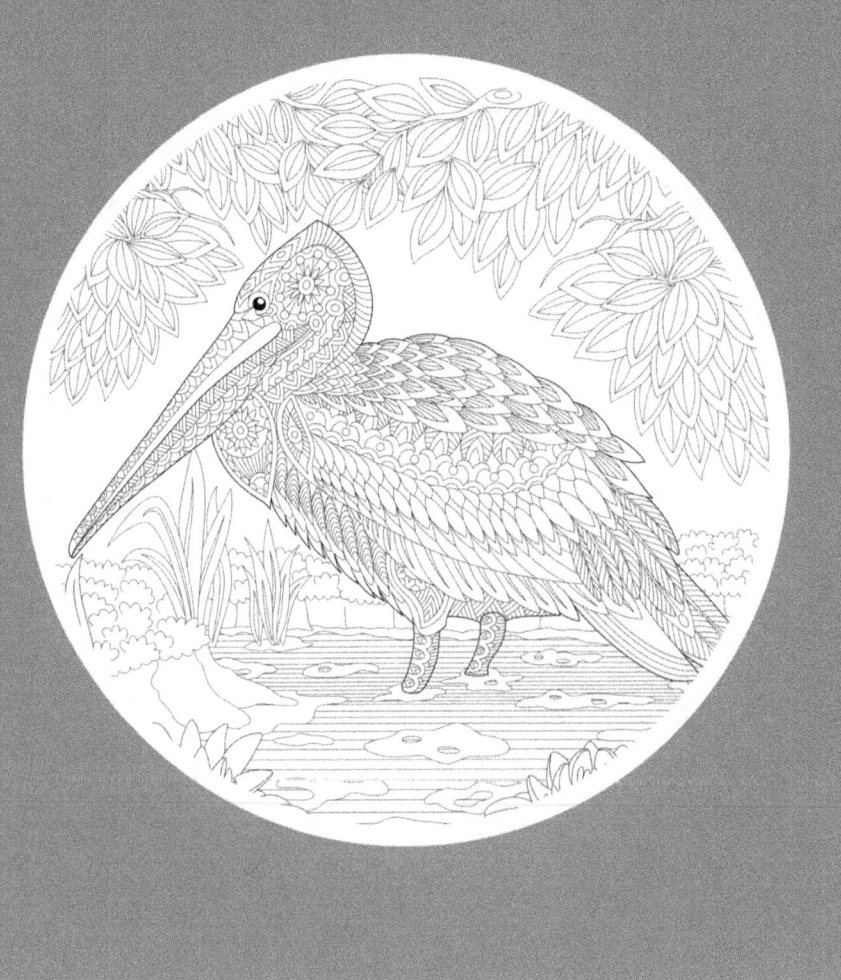

"...I keep looking for one more teacher, only to find that fish learn from the water and birds learn from the sky."

--Mark Nepo

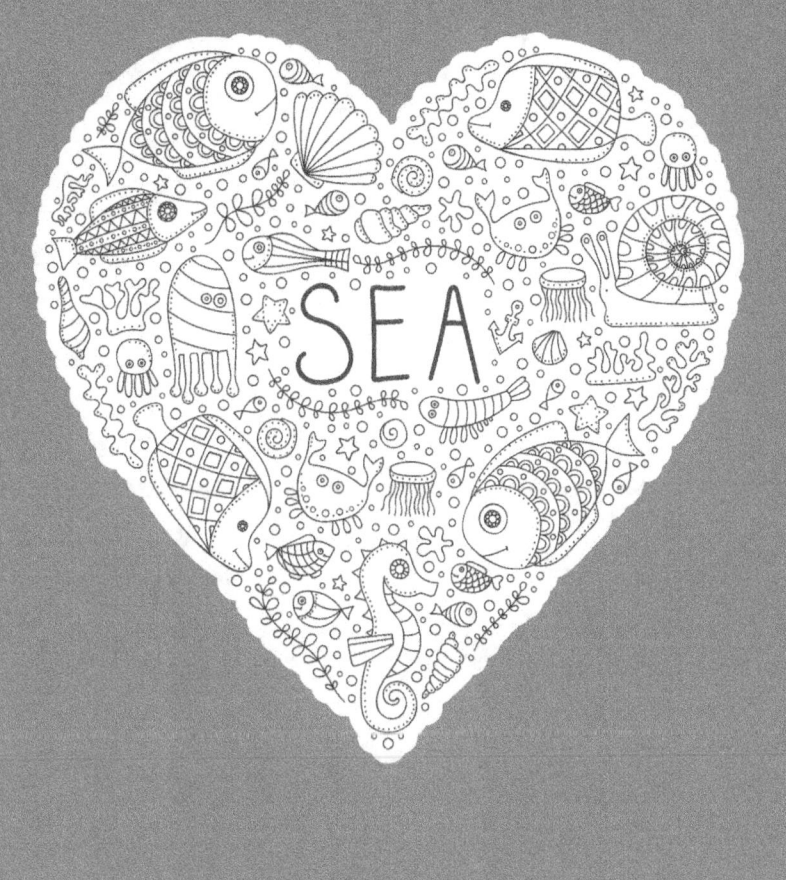

"For whatever we lose (like a you or a me), it's always our self we find in the sea."

--e.e. Cummings

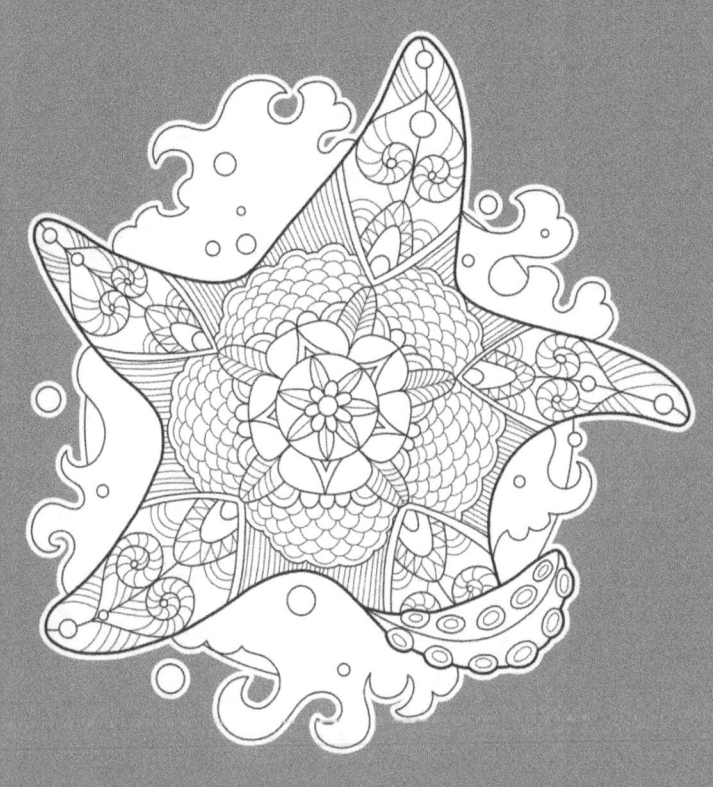

"Your assumptions are your windows on the world. Scrub them off every once in a while, or the light won't come in."

--Isaac Asimov

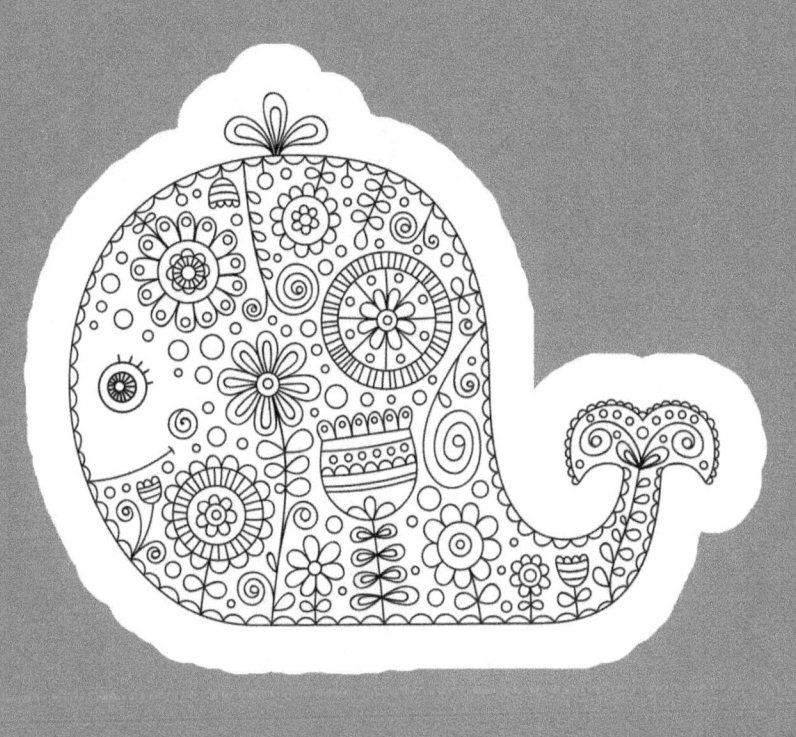

"To have a huge, friendly whale willingly approach your boat and look you straight in the eye is without doubt one of the most extraordinary experiences on the planet."

--Mark Carwardine

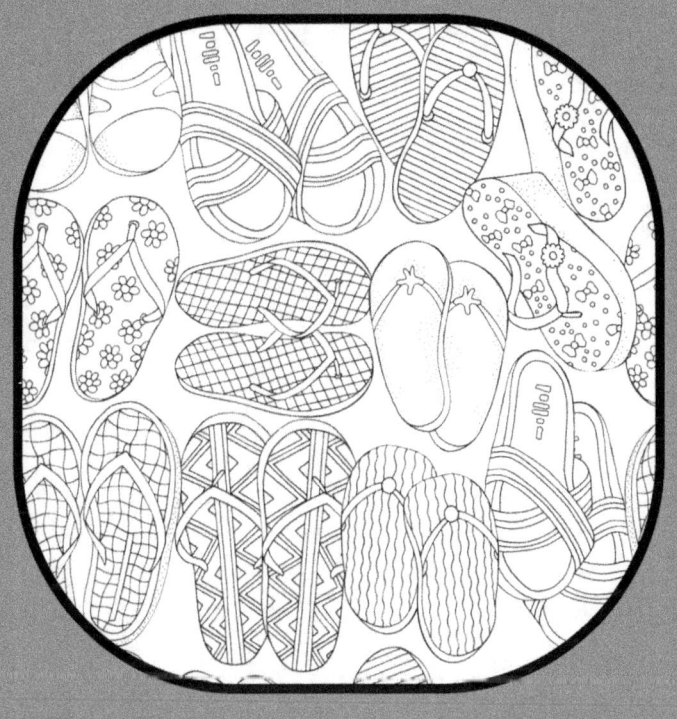

"Never put off till tomorrow what may be done day after tomorrow just as well."

--Mark Twain

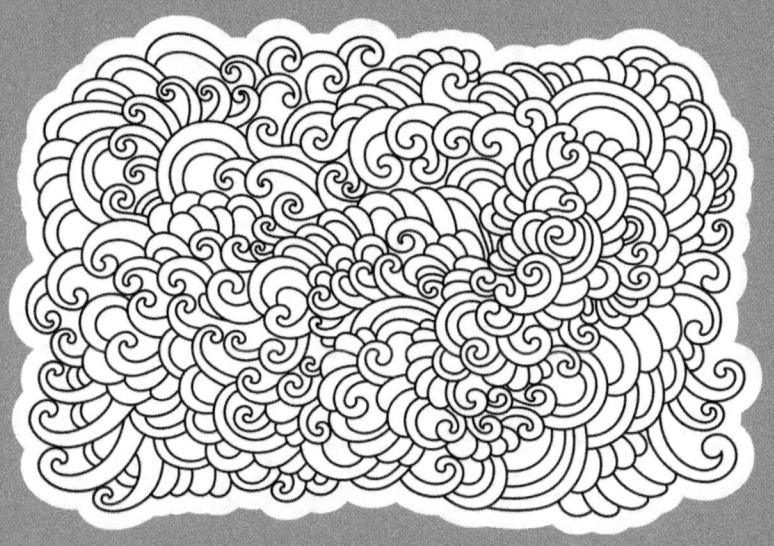

"Don't think about making art, just get it done. Let everyone else decide if it's good or bad, whether they love it or hate it. While they are deciding, make even more art."

--Andy Warhol

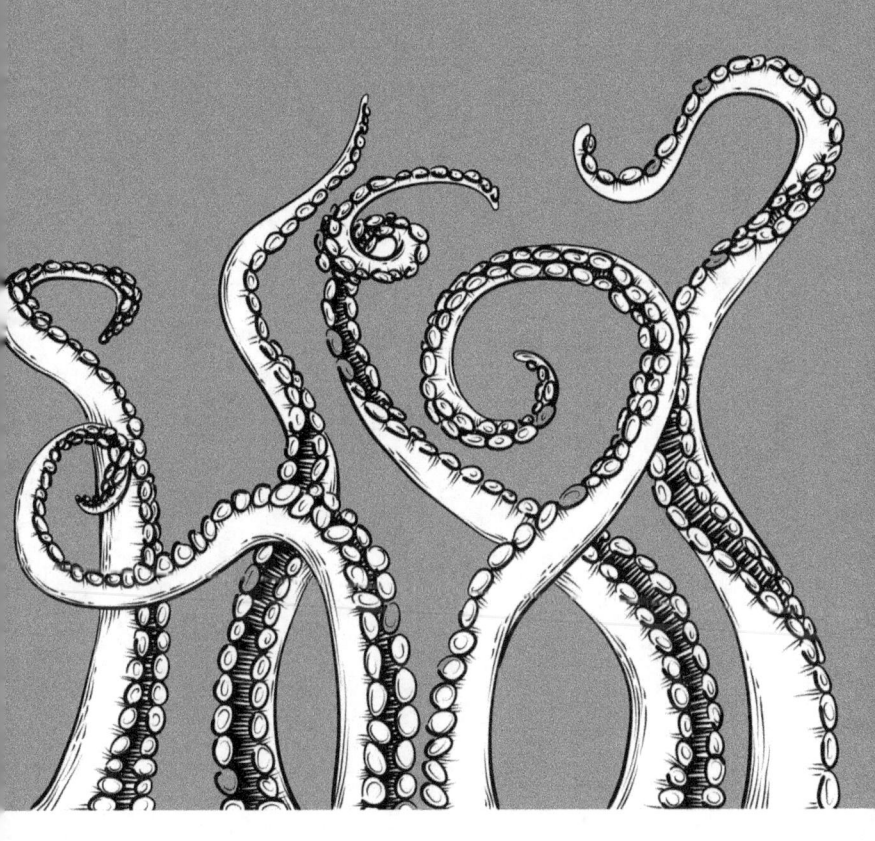

"The difficulty lies not so much in developing new ideas as in escaping from old ones."

--John Maynard Keynes

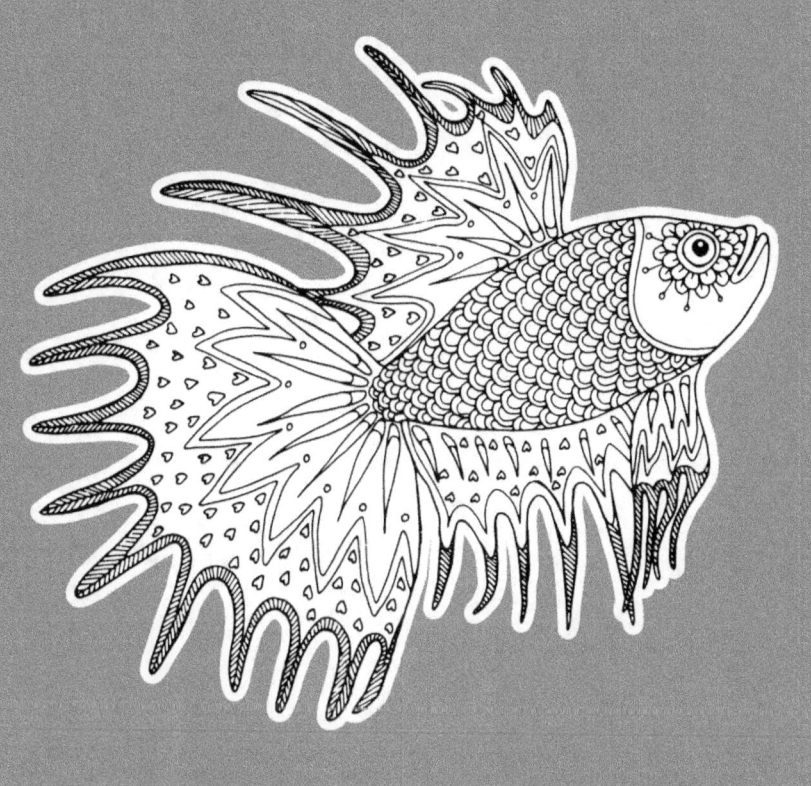

"You only live once, but if you do it right, once is enough."

--Mae West

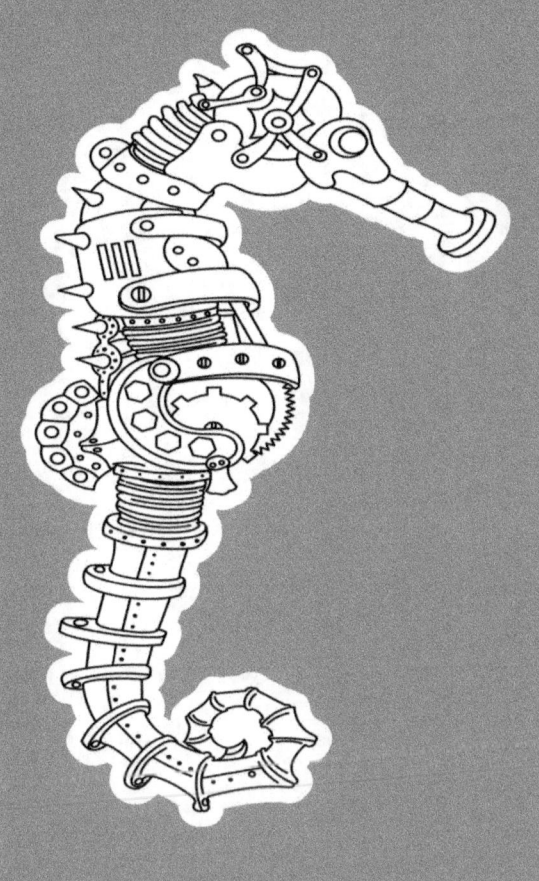

"They deem me mad because I will not sell my days for gold; and I deem them mad because they think my days have a price."

--Khalil Gibran

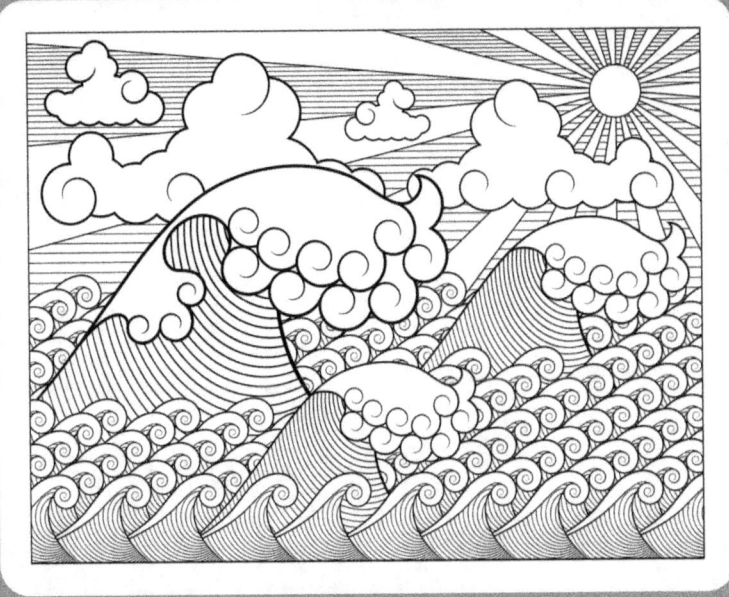

"The waves broke and spread their waters swiftly over the shore. One after another they massed themselves and fell; the spray tossed itself back with the energy of their fall. The waves were steeped deep-blue save for a pattern of diamond-pointed light on their backs which rippled as the backs of great horses ripple with muscles as they move. The waves fell; withdrew and fell again, like the thud of a great beast stamping."

--Virginia Woolf

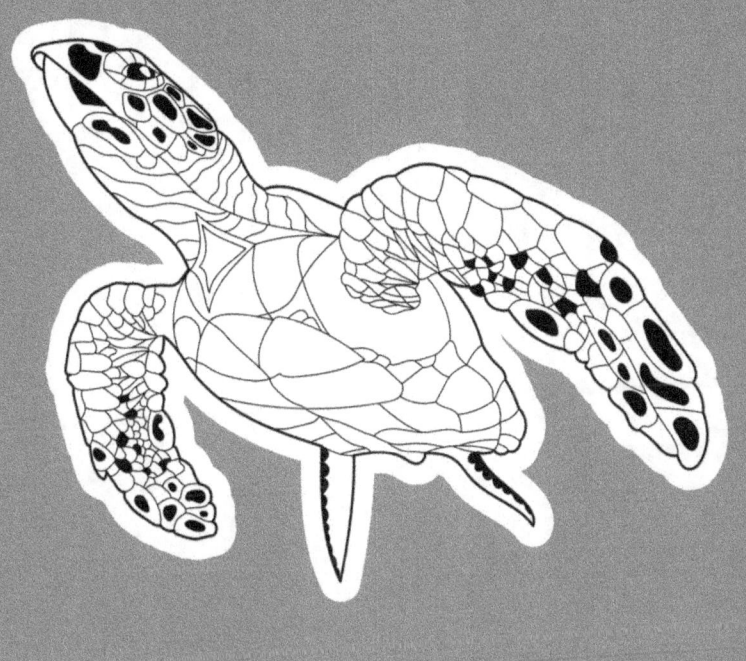

"Watch the turtle. He only moves forward by sticking his neck out."

--Louis V. Gerstner, Jr.

"Do you have an anchor? I have found that a solid anchor is indispensable to one who intends to live life fully. To have an anchor is to be centered and well grounded. It is to have a vital spiritual base."

--Steve Goodier

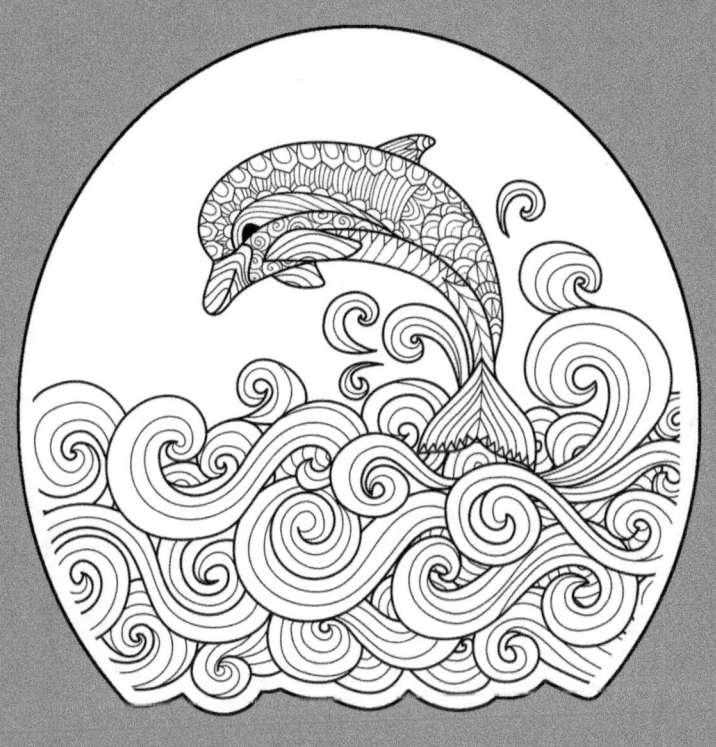

"Though nobody can go back and make a new beginning... Anyone can start over and make a new ending."

--Chico Xavier

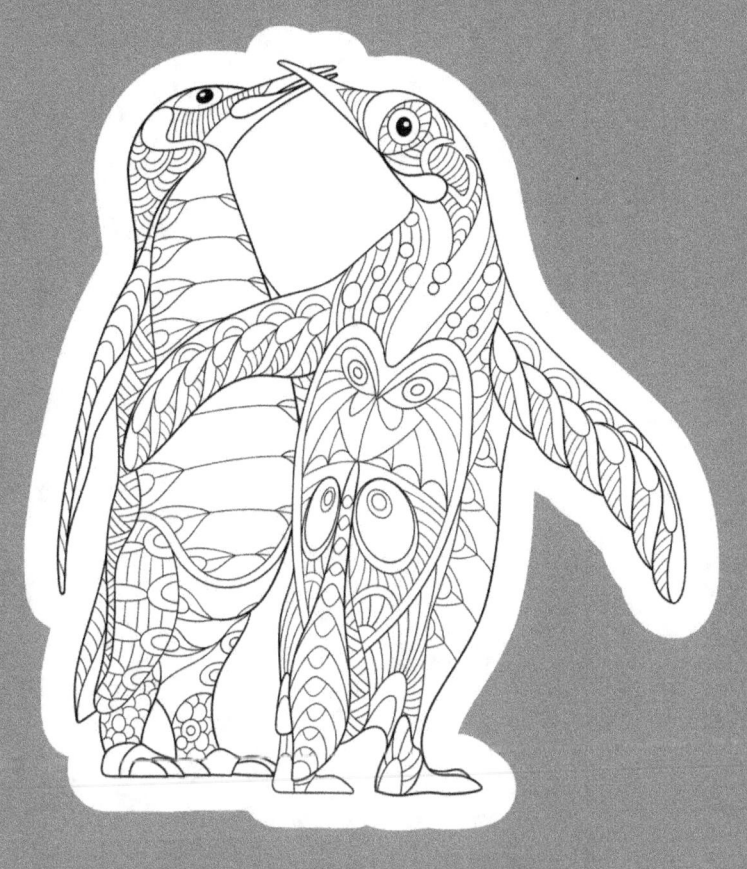

"If Antarctica were music it would be Mozart. Art, and it would be Michelangelo. Literature, and it would be Shakespeare. And yet it is something even greater; the only place on earth that is still as it should be. May we never tame it."

--Andrew Denton

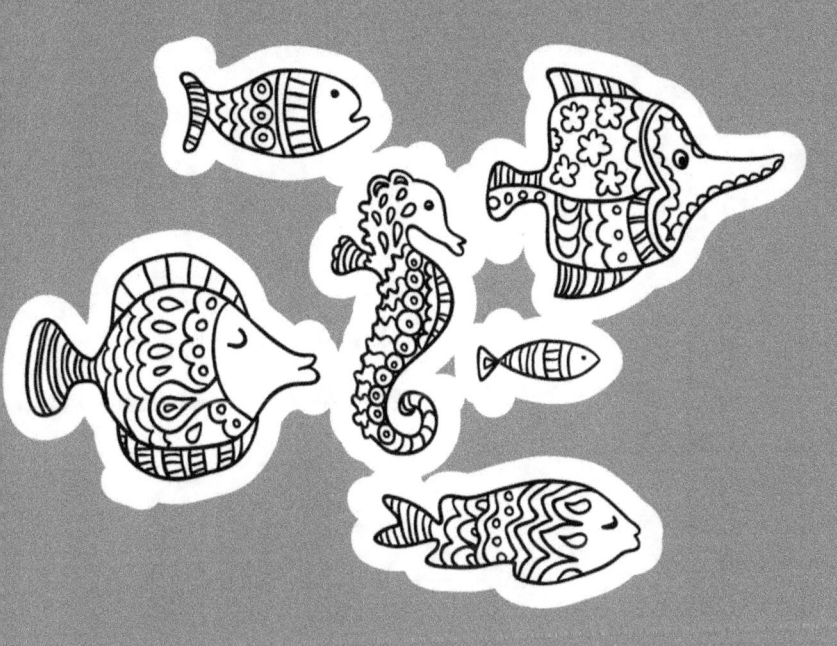

"Something I like to do a lot is just sit by water when there's a current and just stare into the water. I don't fish, I don't hunt, I don't scuba, I don't spear, don't boat, don't play basketball or football - I excel at staring into space. I'm really good at that."

--Iggy Pop

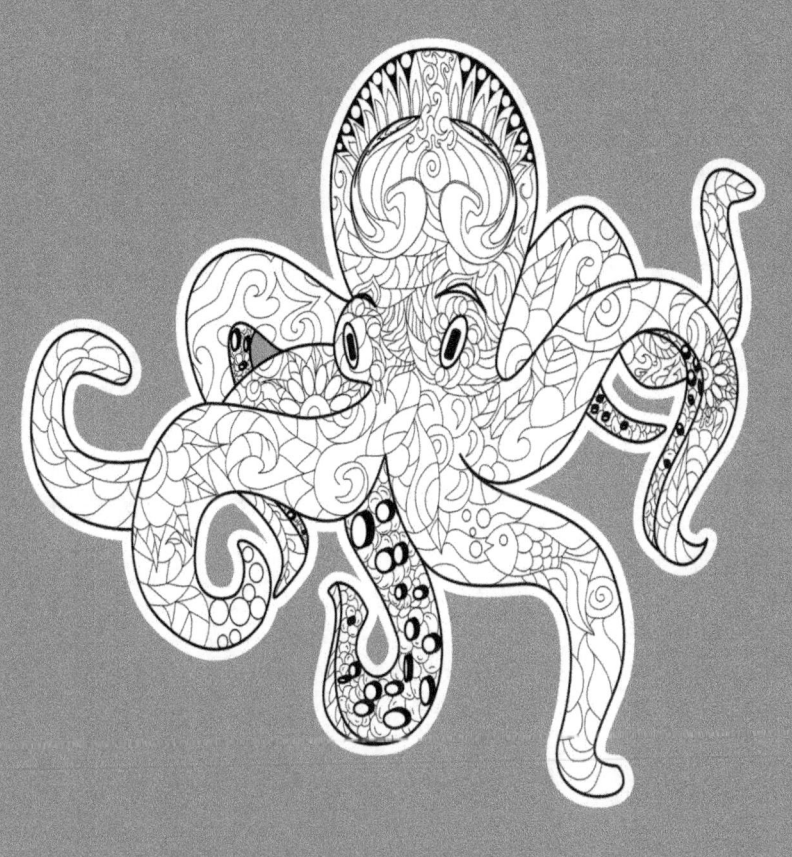

"As my artist's statement explains, my work is utterly incomprehensible and is therefore full of deep significance."

--Calvin and Hobbes

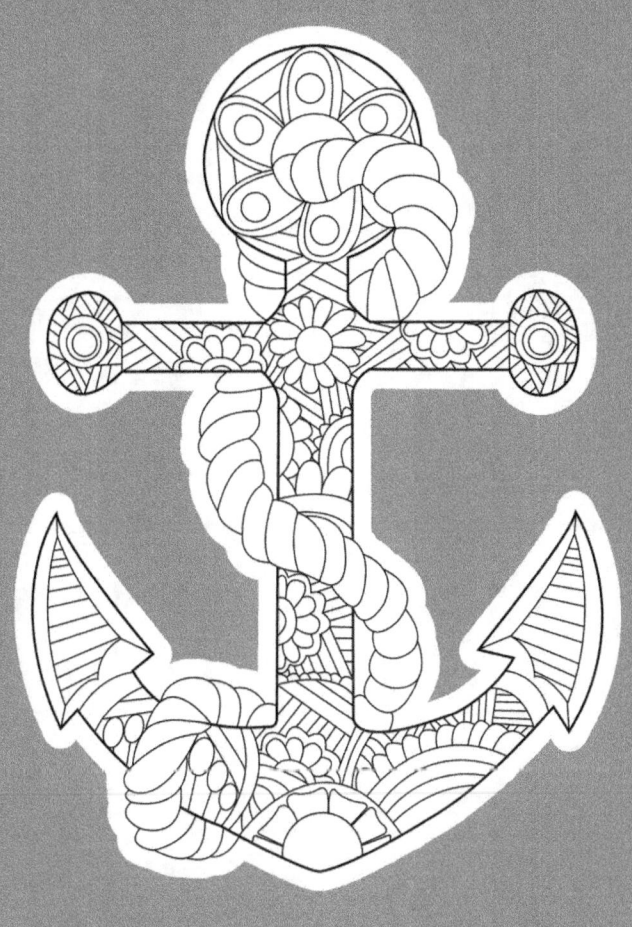

"Finish each day and be done with it. You have done what you could. Some blunders and absurdities no doubt crept in; forget them as soon as you can. Tomorrow is a new day. You shall begin it serenely and with too high a spirit to be encumbered with your old nonsense."

--Ralph Waldo Emerson

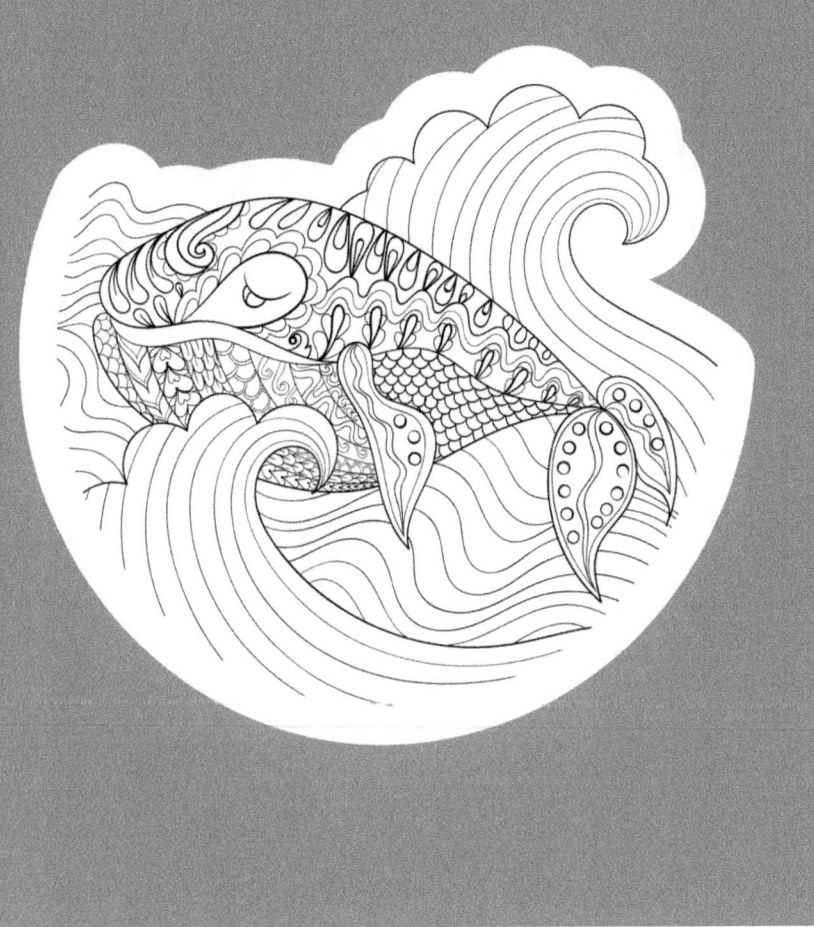

Mason: Dad, there's no real magic in the world, right?

Dad: What do you mean?

Mason: You know, like elves and stuff. People just made that up.

Dad: Oh, I don't know. I mean, what makes you think that elves are any more magical than something like a whale? You know what I mean? What if I told you a story about how underneath the ocean, there was this giant sea mammal that used sonar and sang songs and it was so big that its heart was the size of a car and you could crawl through the arteries? I mean, you'd think that was pretty magical, right?"

--"Boyhood" (Movie; 2014)

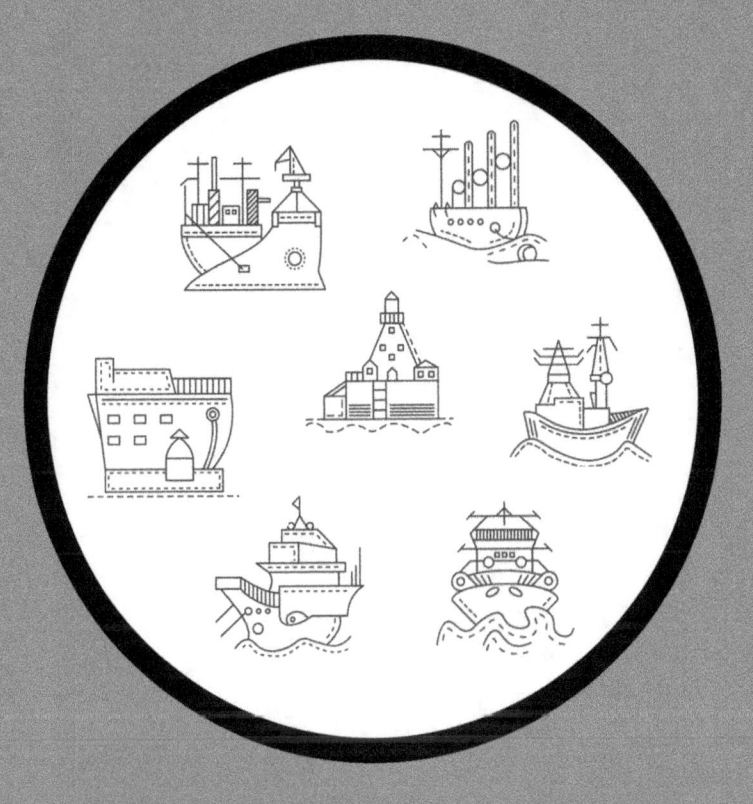

"If you want to build a ship, don't drum up people to collect wood and don't assign them tasks and work, but rather teach them to long for the endless immensity of the sea."

--Antoine de Saint-Exupery

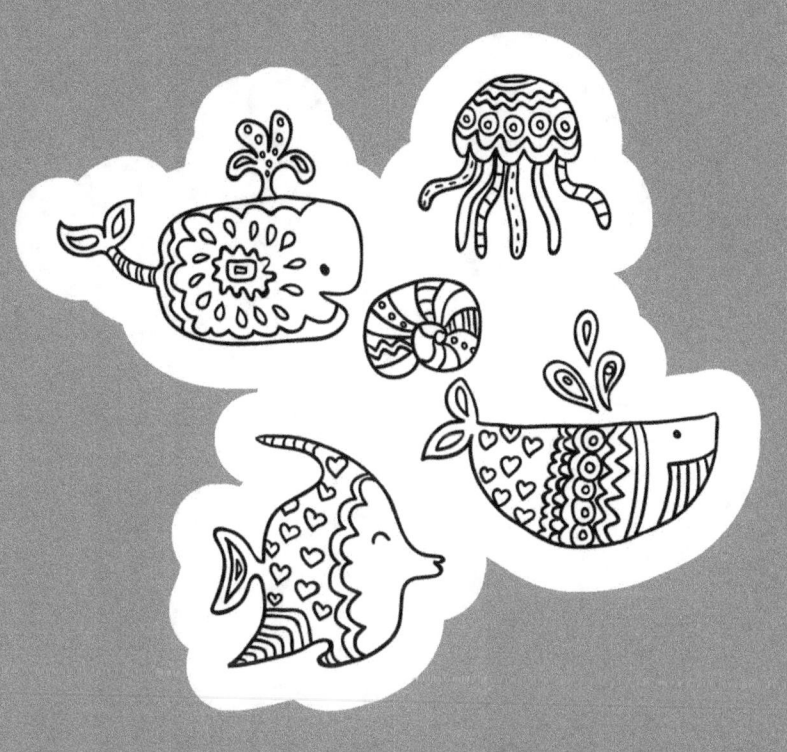

"You must not lose faith in humanity. Humanity is an ocean; if a few drops of the ocean are dirty, the ocean does not become dirty."

--Mahatma Gandhi

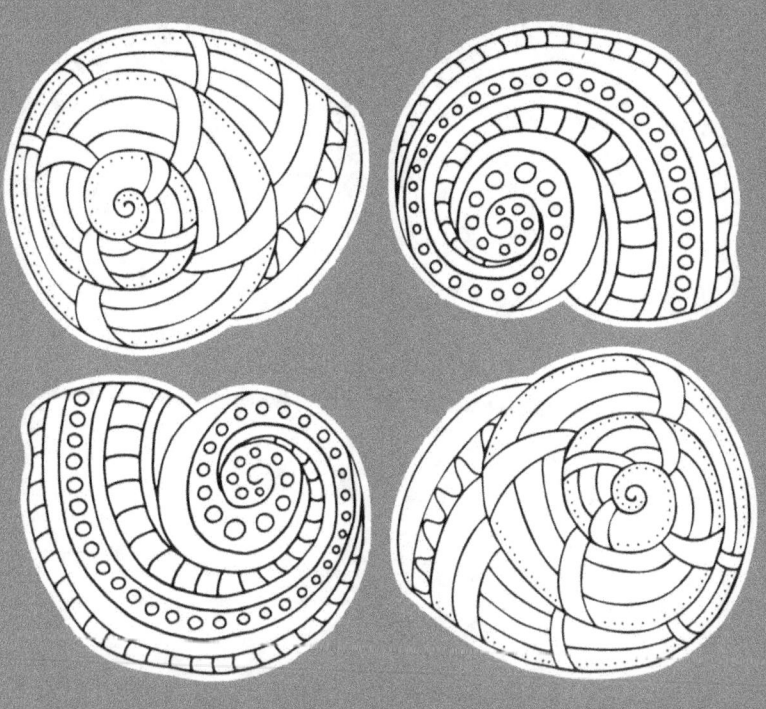

"Go and make interesting mistakes, make amazing mistakes, make glorious and fantastic mistakes. Break rules. Leave the world more interesting for your being here. Make. Good. Art."

--Neil Gaiman

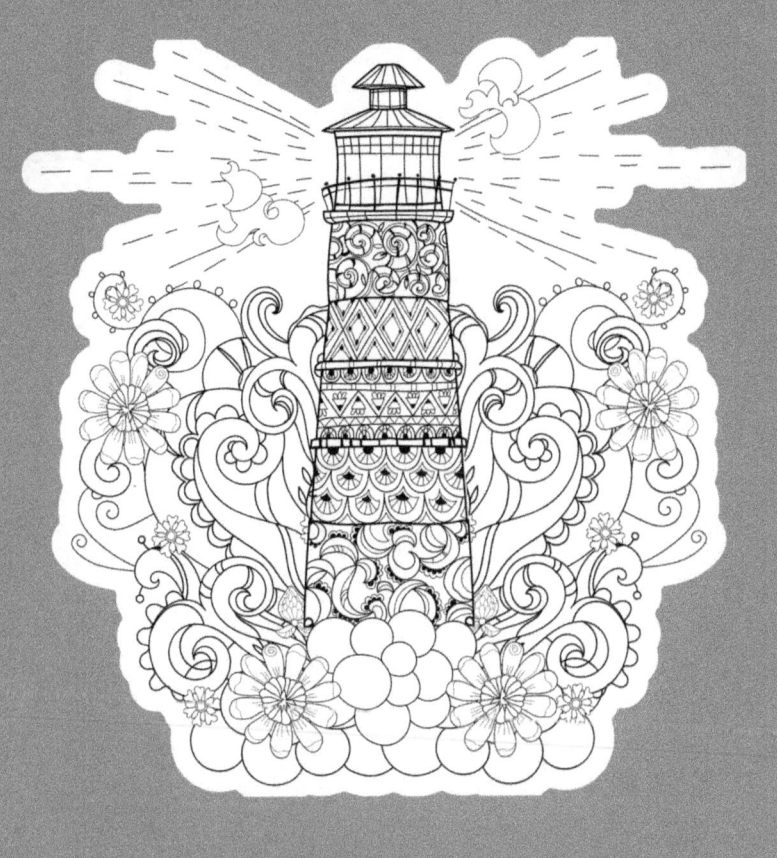

"We are told to let our light shine, and if it does, we won't need to tell anybody it does. Lighthouses don't fire cannons to call attention to their shining - they just shine."

--Dwight L. Moody

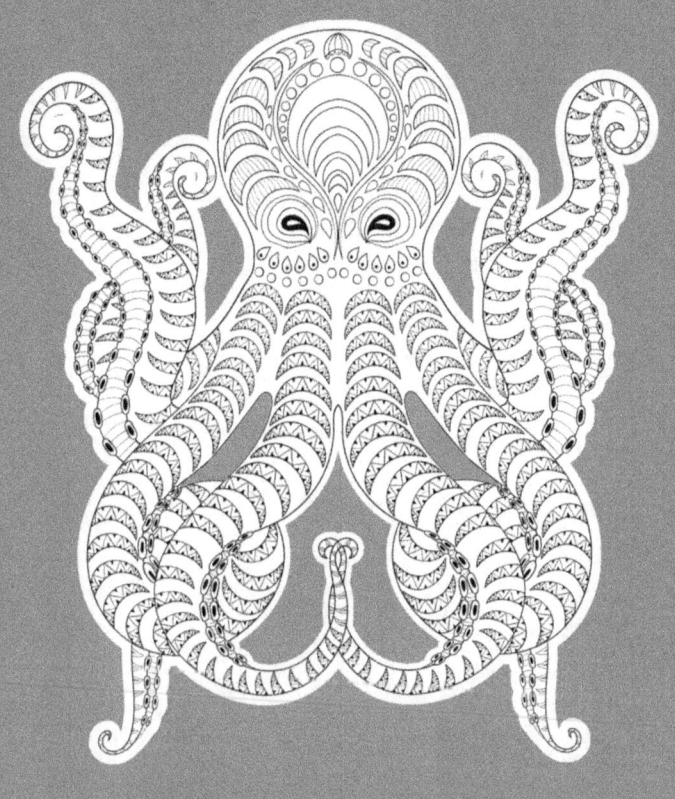

"From 30,000 feet, creating looks like art. From ground level, it's a to-do list."

--Ben Arment

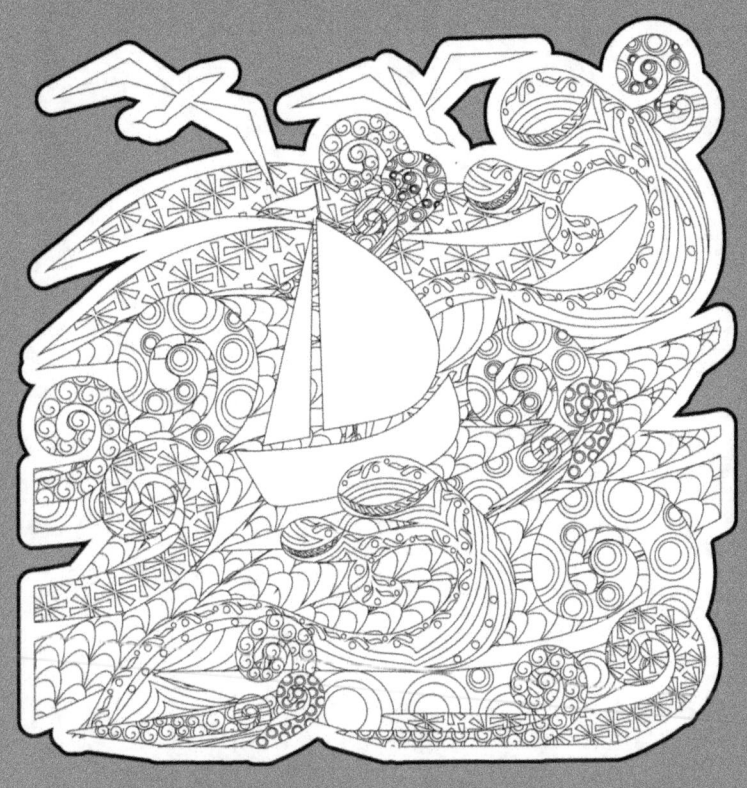

"And once the storm is over, you won't remember how you made it through, how you managed to survive. You won't even be sure, whether the storm is really over. But one thing is certain. When you come out of the storm, you won't be the same person who walked in. That's what this storm's all about."

--Haruki Murakami

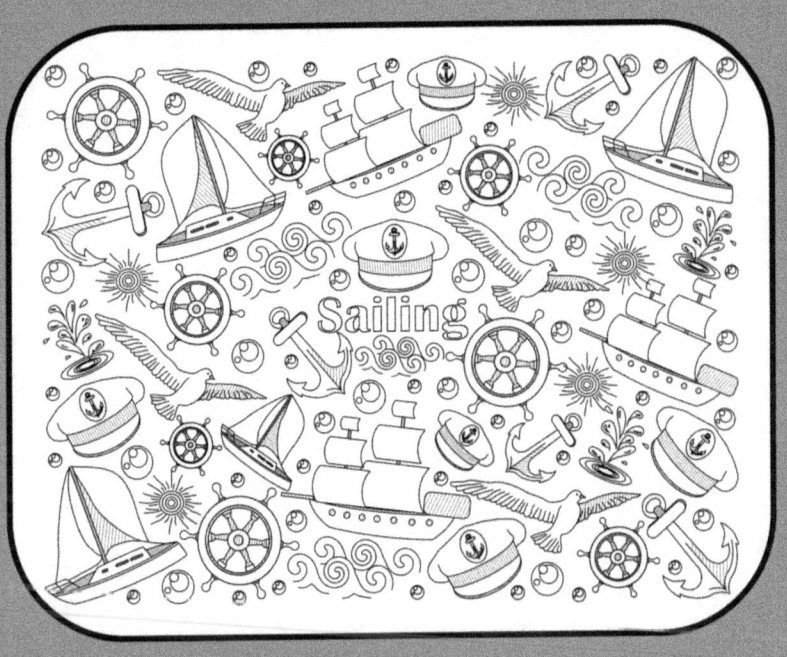

"It's no use waiting for your ship to come in, unless you've sent one out."

--Belgian Proverb

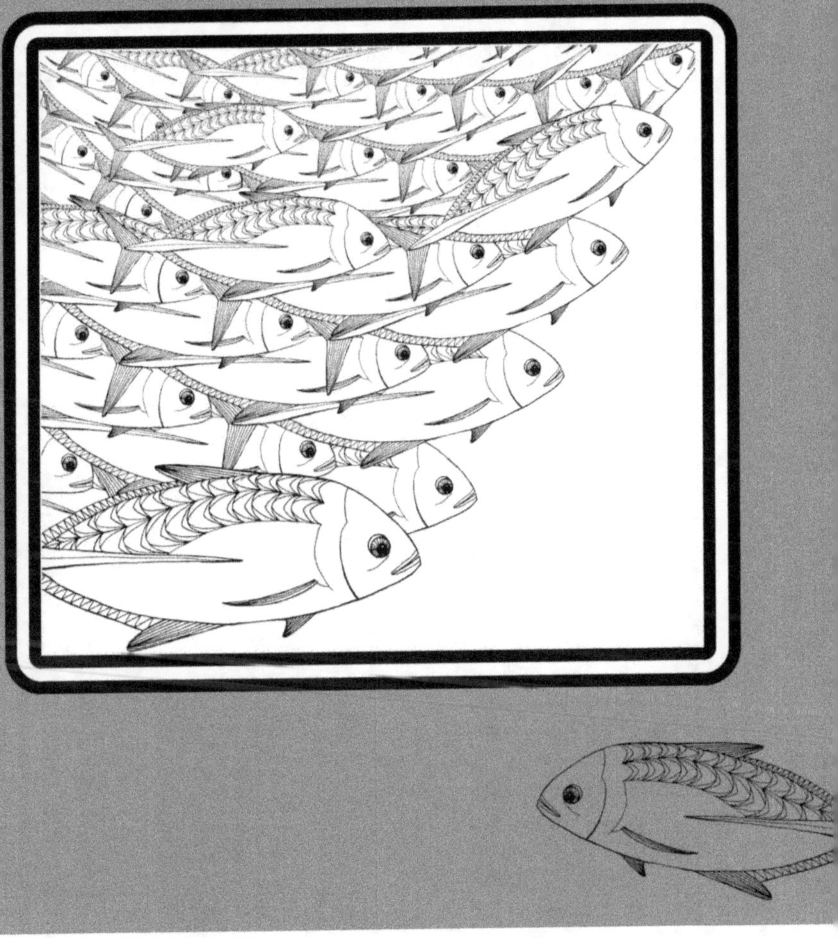

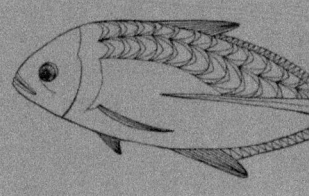

"To go wrong in one's own way is better than to go right in someone else's."

--Fyodor Dostoyevsky

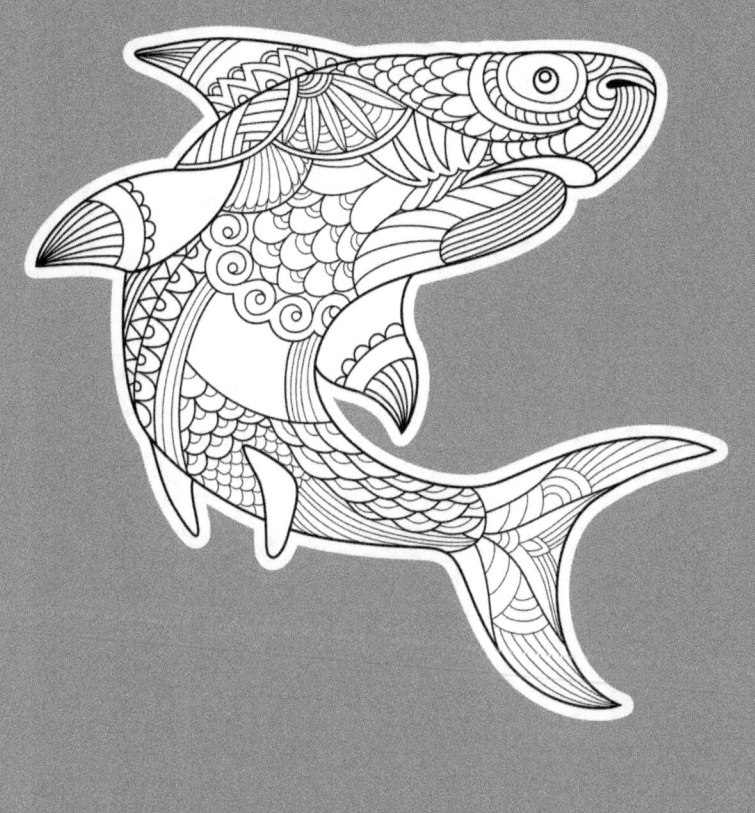

"Life is not measured by the number of breaths we take, but by the moments that take our breath away."

--Maya Angelou

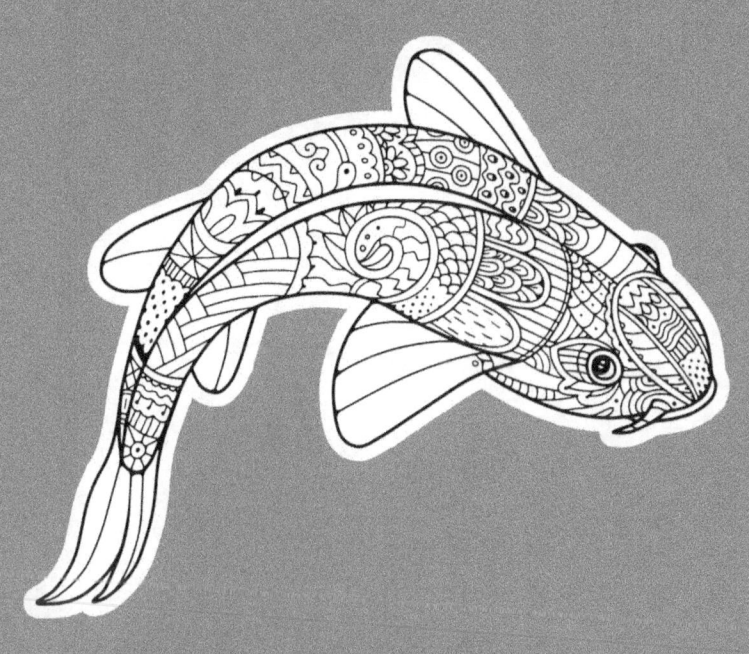

"It may be that when we no longer know what to do, we have come to our real work, and then we no longer know which way to go, we have begun our real journey."

--Wendell Berry

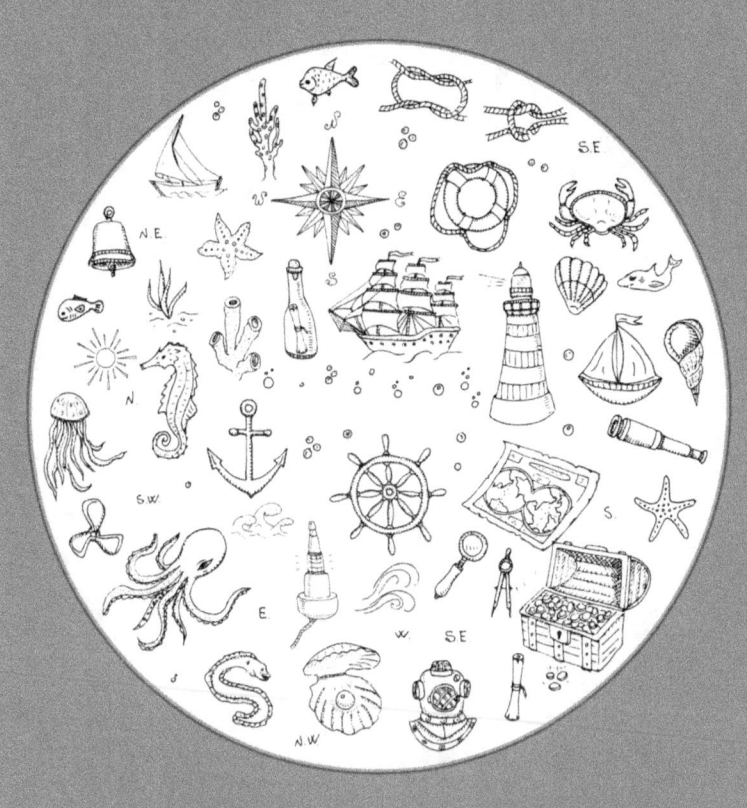

"Just as the wave cannot exist for itself, but is ever a part of the heaving surface of the ocean, so must I never live my life for itself, but always in the experience which is going on around me."

--Albert Schweitzer

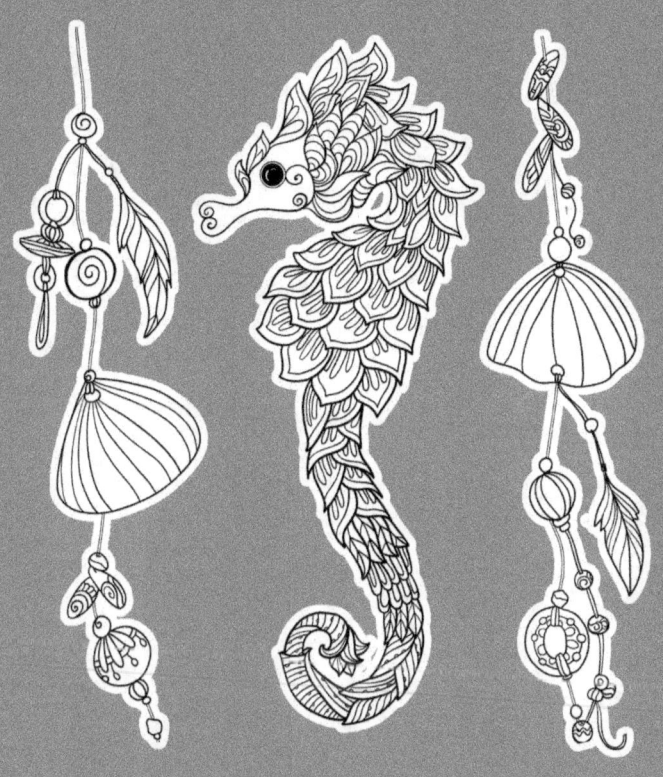

"Sometimes courage is the quiet voice at the end of the day that says I will try again tomorrow."

--Mary Anne Radmacher

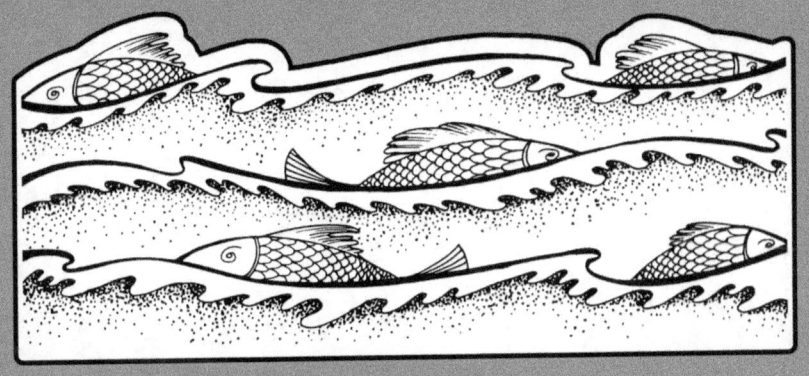

"The fish in the creek said nothing. Fish never do. Few people know what fish think about injustice, or anything else."

--Ursula K. Le Guin

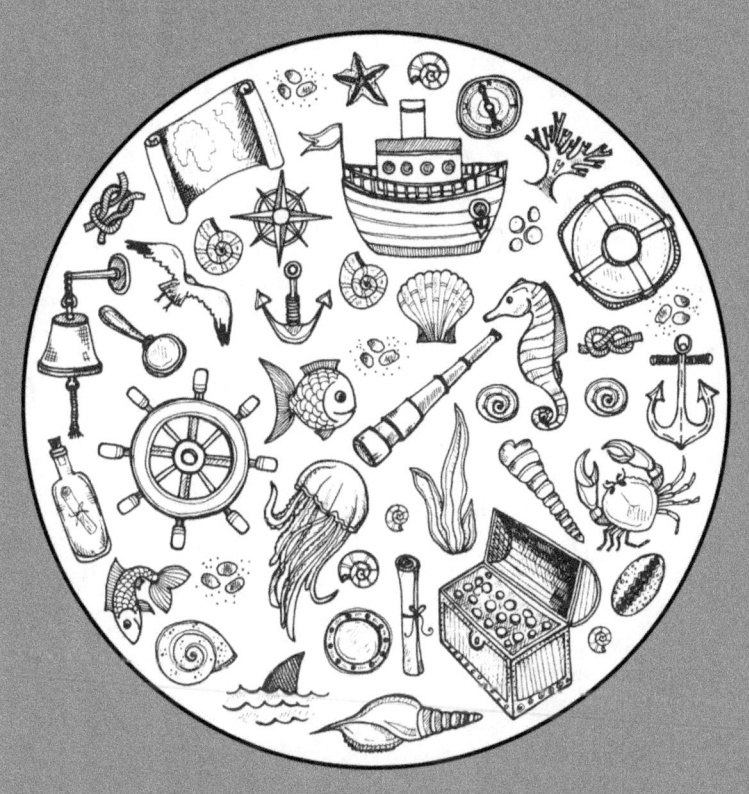

"You cannot discover new oceans unless you have the courage to lose sight of the shore."

--Andre Gide

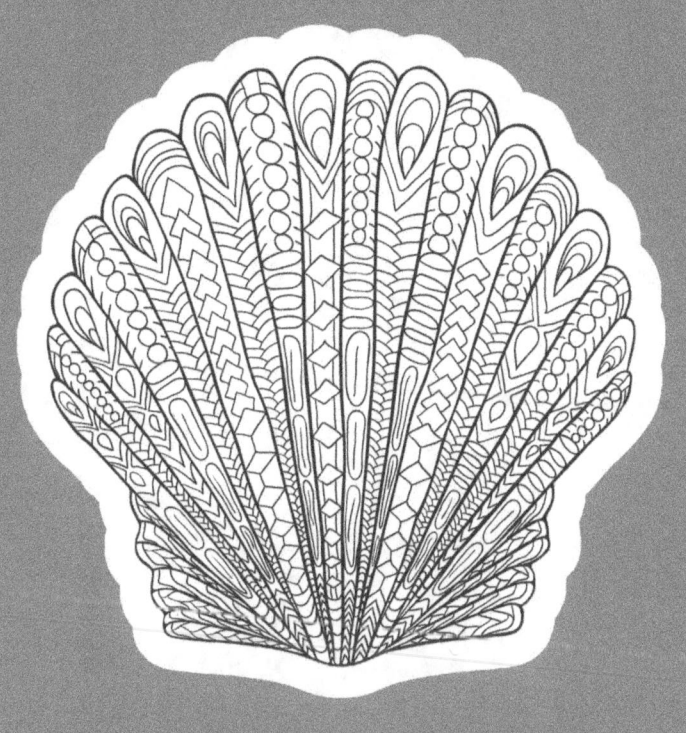

"Thousands of candles can be lit from a single candle, and the life of the candle will not be shortened. Happiness never decreases by being shared."

--Siddhartha Gautama

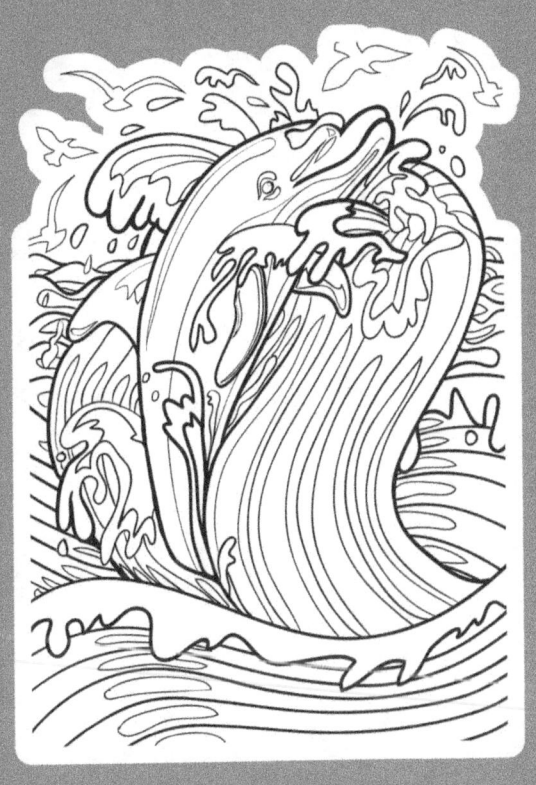

"Instead of worrying about what you cannot control, shift your energy to what you can create."

--Roy T. Bennett

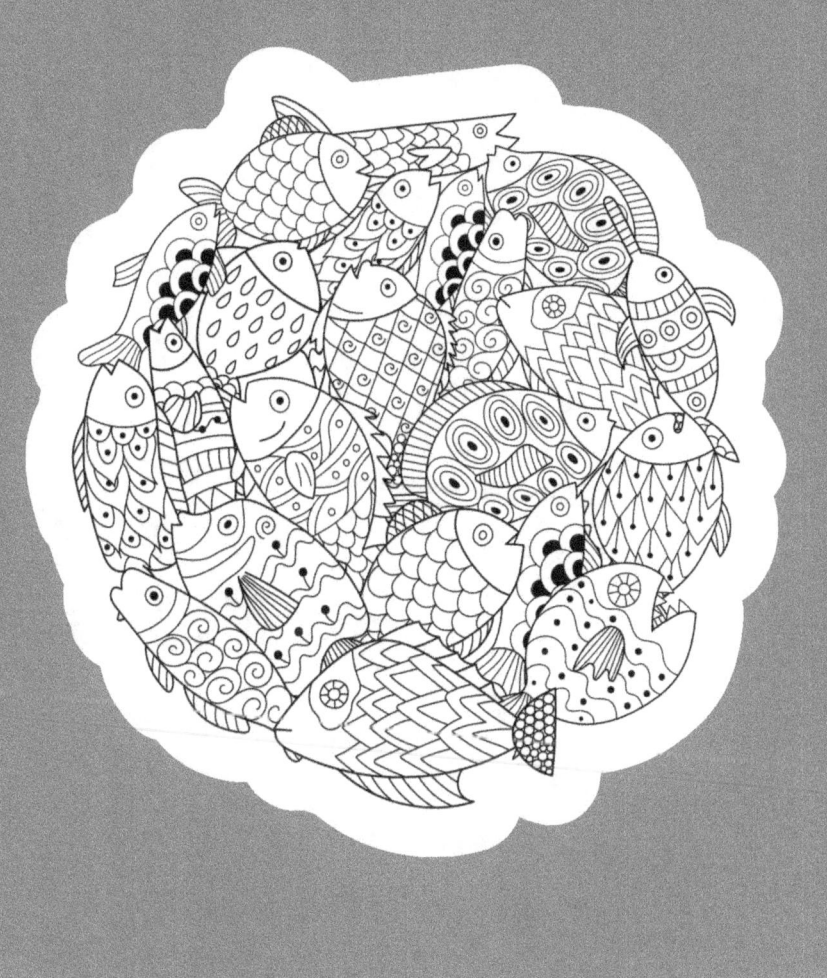

"The sea is emotion incarnate. It loves, hates, and weeps. It defies all attempts to capture it with words and rejects all shackles. No matter what you say about it, there is always that which you can't."

--Christopher Paolini

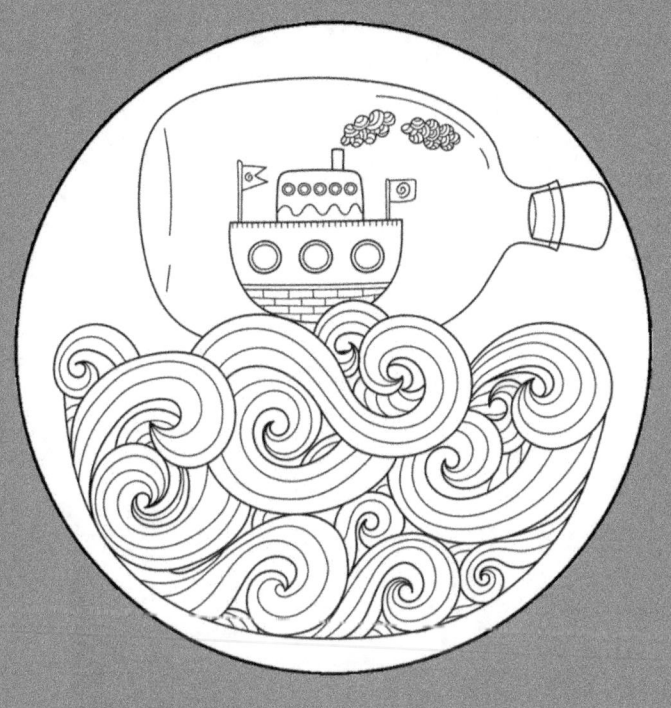

"Don't cry because it's over, smile because it happened."

--Dr. Seuss